AROUND THE WORLD

STEAM SUPERPOWER

AROUND THE WORLD

R. K. EVANS C.Eng. F.I.Mech.E.

BRADFORD BARTON

Frontispiece: Acme of steam locomotive development: a Union Pacific 'Big Boy' 4-8-8-4, one of a class of 25 simple-articulated, 540-ton giants that held down freight service across Wyoming and Utah from their introduction in 1941 until the autumn of 1958.

© copyright D. Bradford Barton 1976 □ ISBN 0 85153 209 8 □ Set in Times and printed by offset litho by H. E. Warne Ltd, London and St. Austell, for the publishers D. Bradford Barton Ltd, Trethellan House, Truro, Cornwall

introduction

Two commemorative events, an ocean apart, in the summer of 1975 saw the return to operation of two steam locomotives which truly exemplified the term Superpower. In June and July, Southern Pacific Lines' 4449, a streamlined 4-8-4 resplendent in red, blue and silver that for sixteen years had stood on display in a Portland, Oregon park, travelled in steam 3300 miles across the United States to head the bicentennial 'American Freedom Train'; and in August, 92220 *Evening Star,* the 2-10-0 that was the last steam engine built for British Railways, made a nostalgic if less spectacular journey from Shildon to Darlington as part of the Steam Cavalcade commemorating the opening of the Stockton & Darlington Railway 150 years before.

Defining Superpower in terms of those two locomotives indicates very clearly the parallel paths of engineering design and development that marked the final years of steam: the ubiquitous 4-8-4 that represented, beneath its glamorised exterior, the modern North American general-purpose locomotive, designed and built by one of a thriving triumvirate of private builders and incorporating components from a hundred more; and the 2-10-0 that distilled the experience of four pre-nationalisation railways into a simple, standardised locomotive built, to the last cotter-pin and rivet, to the designs and in the workshops of the railway that was to operate it. To the American engineer and railfan, the term Superpower is specific: it was coined by the Lima Locomotive Corporation in 1925 to describe its pioneer 2-8-4 demonstrator A-1, the engine that, as flagbearer of the high steaming-capacity, high-horsepower era, had unmatched influence on the following quarter-century of steam locomotive design. The engines that powered US railroads through the depression years, through World War 2 and into the diesel age were predominantly 2-8-4s, 2-10-4s and 4-8-4s designed on the Superpower principles embodied in A-1 and promoted by Lima until the last months of steam construction.

To the European enthusiast, the superpower concept was broader in application; it embraced, in general, locomotives which were in advance of their time in respect not only of horsepower but of tractive effort and maximum speed and, latterly, of the high availability and ease of maintenance typified by *Evening Star*. For this book, similarly, I have selected locomotives which exemplified the broader theme of superpower: designs which, in the context of time and place, represented a major technical advance on their predecessors. In comparing and describing their features I have adopted the widely-understood units of tractive effort and drawbar horsepower; weights and dimensions are expressed in their most commonly-accepted form. Remember, though, that criteria of power and capacity—and the means of measuring them—can vary widely within a single administration, and internationally even more so.

Few countries experienced identical conditions of terrain and climate, and in turn the variety of locomotive designs in use throughout the world at a given period reflected geographical and operating requirements more than technical refinement: it was no coincidence that the final steam locomotives to remain in use as a railway system turned to diesel traction were often the simpler, older types with low maintenance costs and wide availability.

Nor was it coincidence that railway engineers the world over eschewed the adoption of technically-superior features—high-pressure and water-tube boilers, condensing turbines, electric transmission, for example—and remained faithful instead to the firetube boiler, two or at most four cylinders, and simple reciprocating drive. Certain refinements did, indeed, see a vogue under individual engineers: compounding, for example, was almost a trademark of design practice in France, where fuel was sufficiently expensive to outweigh the extra maintenance costs incurred; and multiple, simple-expansion cylinders typified practice in Britain, where the loading gauge precluded the incorporation of two cylinders and valves large enough to produce the power required. Elsewhere, certainly in the United States and much of Europe, accessibility and reliability were accorded higher priority than thermal efficiency and low fuel consumption. Similarly, valve design in general followed the mainstream of reciprocating piston valves actuated by Walschaerts or Baker gear; poppet valves, despite their advantages of absorbing relatively little drive power and permitting independent inlet and exhaust events, were common only in France, Italy and Spain.

Boiler and firebox design, again, favoured the basic simplicity of the Stephenson firetube boiler throughout 125 years of locomotive development. Changes were evolutionary rather than revolutionary, including the introduction of arch tubes and thermic syphons, welded in place of riveted joints, self-cleaning smokeboxes, and rocking grates and hopper ashpans. High boiler pressures—250lb/in² and above—were occasionally adopted, at the cost of increased maintenance, and watertube-boiler experiments had a brief vogue on many railways but usually ended their days rebuilt in conventional form. One such boiler, the Yarrow three-drum unit originally built in 1929 for H. N. Gresley's 4-6-4 No. 10000, spent a useful 20-year working life after the engine's rebuilding in 1938—as a stationary testing facility at Stooperdale boiler shops, Darlington, where its nominal 450lb/in² pressure was ideal for steam-testing repaired boilers before their despatch to the North Road erecting shops.

Two 20th-century developments did make a major contribution to steam locomotive technology, and to our story of superpower: the theoretical study of steam circuit design by André Chapelon in France, and its practical application in the improved draughting, higher superheat and streamlined steam ports and passages that transformed European locomotive performance from 1930 onwards; and the evolution of articulated locomotives, as originally envisaged by Anatole Mallet in 1884 and H. W. Garratt in 1909, into the biggest, heaviest and most powerful examples of steam engines ever built. Garratt's brainchild carved out its legendary career predominantly in Africa, where even today many hundreds of Beyer-Garratts remain in active service in Rhodesia, Kenya and the Republic. In the United States, the Mallet compound evolved into the simple-articulated giants that saw out the final years of steam, such as the Chesapeake & Ohio 2-6-6-6s which on test produced close to 7500 drawbar horsepower, and the Missabe Road's 2-8-8-4s that handled the world's heaviest trains, iron-ore extras grossing 18,000 tons.

Ultimate expression of the modern superpower theme took effect in North America—relatively unaffected by World War 2—during the 1940's, and in Europe between 1935 and the early 1950's, by which time almost every railway administration was committed to alternative forms of traction.

Certain characteristics were common to the final flowering of steam power on both sides of the Atlantic; many of them were developed primarily to aid availability, which was already the strongest card in the diesel salesman's hand—such features included roller bearings on all axles, coupling and connecting rods and valve gear; self-cleaning smokeboxes and rocking grates to speed turnround at the end of a trip; and lineside or on-board water-treatment equipment that virtually overcame the problems of boiler corrosion and scaling. Their effectiveness can best be recalled by a year-long series of comparative trials between six New York Central 4-8-4s, built by ALCO in 1946, and six diesels of equivalent power. During the tests, carried out on the principal expresses between Chicago and Harmon, New York, the Northerns' availability averaged 76 per cent—equal to that of the competing diesels—and their annual mileage averaged 314,700, equivalent to 862 miles daily.

In Europe, meanwhile, the onset of full-scale diesel and electric traction was delayed by the cost of recovering from the war, and steam power in Britain, Germany and France had an extended lease of life over its North American counterpart. Particularly noteworthy were the designs of André Chapelon in France, including a three-cylinder compound 4-8-4 which matched the power output of the Pennsylvania T1 duplex from a grate area a little over half the size and at a specific fuel consumption some 20 per cent less; and one of the British standardised designs, the two-cylinder 2-10-0 which was ultimately multiplied to a total of 251 locomotives. Eastern Europe, too, continued to develop outstanding steam designs well into the 1950's, notably in Czechoslovakia.

Several representative European and U.S. locomotives of the postwar period are illustrated in the following pages; that their working lives were so short, in some cases no more than five years, is due less to any shortcomings in design than to the concerted sales attack of the diesel makers. In the United States, even as the steam giants of the 1940's were being designed and built, ALCO, Fairbanks-Morse and Electro-Motive demonstrators were touring the nation's rails signalling their end; the beginning of that decade saw 800 diesels facing the ranks of more than 40,000 steam locomotives, yet within ten years the steam erecting shops at Eddystone, Schenectady and Lima were closed and the story of steam superpower had reached its final chapter.

GREAT BRITAIN: simplicity the keynote

For more than a century, the dominant characteristic of British locomotive design was elegance rather than power. To many railway mechanical engineers, from Webb to Bulleid, economy of construction and ease of maintenance were subjugated to aesthetics; sheer power, in any event, was seldom necessary in a country where trains were light and frequent, and in which platform and siding length dictated train weight more than did a locomotive's haulage capacity.

Within the limits of Britain's restrictive loading gauge, nonetheless, some outstanding locomotives were designed and built, commonly for ultra-high speeds, for use on steep gradients or, in at least one notable case—James Holden's Great Eastern Railway 0-10-0 tank of 1902—for rapid acceleration in intensive commuter service. By the 1930's, all four post-Grouping companies had eliminated the least successful of the locomotives inherited from their predecessors; on at least two of them, the best of overseas design principles were being combined with major developments in their own drawing-offices to produce locomotives destined to see out the steam era some 40 years later. The A4 and 'Coronation' Pacifics of Nigel Gresley and William Stanier, respectively, set unparalleled standards of performance on the main lines to Scotland, both owing much to the work of André Chapelon in their streamlined steam passages and multiple cylinders.

Compounding found little favour in Britain, the last compound locomotive, a Smith-system 4-4-0, being built in 1932. Occasional attempts to achieve superpower through high boiler pressures proved impractical, and such locomotives as Gresley's water-tube boiler 4-6-4 and the LMS 4-6-0 *Fury* were soon converted to conventional form. Other aids to performance were introduced, generally without results sufficiently outstanding to justify their wide application. Booster engines, for example, though tried on passenger locomotives, were perpetuated only on hump shunters; and the various forms of poppet valves installed on isolated locomotives had little effect on the almost universal application of long-lap, long-travel piston valves actuated by Walschaerts gear.

Beyer-Garratt locomotives met with success in two specific roles—hauling heavy coal trains between Toton, near Nottingham, and north London; and in banking service on the Worsborough incline, on the former Great Central route across the Pennines. The 72,900lb tractive effort of Gresley's unique six-cylinder 2-8-8-2, built for the latter duty in 1925 and remaining active for 30 years, assured its place as Britain's most powerful locomotive.

Culmination of British express-passenger design was Sir Nigel Gresley's three-cylinder A4 Pacific of 1935. Thirty-four lasted into British Railways days: *Falcon* and *Dominion of New Zealand* are here ready to head expresses out of Kings Cross for the north.

o European 4-6-0 ever exceeded the tractive
fort of C. B. Collett's Great Western 'King'
ass, the first of which, *King George V,* ap-
eared in 1927 and was immediately shipped to
merica to take part in the Centenary celebra-
ons of the Baltimore & Ohio Railroad. Four 16
28in cylinders, 78in wheels and 250lb boiler
ressure combined to produce a designed tractive
rce of 40,300lb.

First British Pacific, Churchward's *The Great Bear* of 1908,
was soon converted to a 4-6-0: it fell to H. N. Gresley to
introduce the first successful 4-6-2 with his *Great Northern* of
1922. Forty years later, Gresley's A3s were still in top-link
passenger service, witness 60074 *Harvester* heading a Leeds
express through Hessle Quarry.

11

Finest of all Sir William Stanier's locomotives for the LMS were his 38 four-cylinder 'Coronation' Pacifics. In May 1963, her last month of service, *Queen Elizabeth* is set to leave Glasgow with the southbound 'Royal Scot'.

Unique high-pressure experiment was Gresley's four-cylinder compound 4-6-4 No. 10000 of 1929, carrying a 450lb three-drum watertube boiler. Heavy on coal and maintenance, the engine was rebuilt in 1938 as a three-cylinder simple with conventional, 250lb boiler. As 60700, Britain's last-remaining Hudson continued in main-line service until 1959; it is here leaving York with a Kings Cross express.

ain's most powerful
eam: Gresley's
3-2 Garratt 69999 at
on works.

-produced freight
es of World War 2
R. A. Riddles'
erity 2-10-0s (at
erwell, left) and
s (at Hessle Quarry
e winter of 1955).

16 Sir Henry Fowler's original 'Royal Scot' 4-6-0s of 1927 were multiplied to a total of 70 engines; as rebuilt by Stanier with new cylinders and coned boilers, all survived into postwar days. In June 1957, footplate crews change as *The Loyal Regiment* pauses at Hereford with a Plymouth-Manchester train.

Ireland's Great Southern Railway main line between Dublin and Cork was the unlikely domain of E. C. Bredin's three Class B1a three-cylinder 4-6-0s; after the GWR 'Kings' they were Europe's most powerful 4-6-0s. All were named after Irish Queens; 802 *Tailte* is seen at Cork in April 1954.

WESTERN EUROPE: the two schools of design

Steam locomotive development in continental Europe was spearheaded by the railways of France and Germany; other countries, such as Belgium and Italy, supplied many design features—the Belpaire firebox, Walschaerts and Caprotti valve gear, the Zara truck, for example—but it was to French and German practice that the world's railway engineers looked for large-scale innovation.

In Germany, even after unification of the seven state systems in 1920, the influence of the Prussian State Railway remained dominant, many of its 25,000 locomotives still being in use throughout Europe for the next 50 years. During the 1920's and 1930's Reichsbahn engineers, under Dr R. P. Wagner and working closely with the major builders such as Henschel and Krupp, developed a series of standardised two-cylinder, simple-expansion locomotives able to serve the needs of the entire country; as in the similar British standardisation programme of the 1950's, component interchangeability and ease of maintenance were given high priority. For the largest engines, three and (in two Pacific designs) four cylinders were incorporated, and construction of the 29 classes continued until 1939, culminating in the magnificent Type 06 4-8-4 and Type 45 2-10-2 designs produced shortly before the outbreak of war.

Parallel with this mainstream of standardisation, the introduction of ultra-high speed services in the mid-1930's initiated further designs. Type 05, two engines built by Borsig in 1934, were streamlined three-cylinder 4-6-4s with driving wheels of 7ft 6in diameter; a third member of the class was fueled with pulverised coal and operated with the cab leading. High-speed tank engines were also built, including a unique three-cylinder 4-6-6T also carried on 7ft 6in coupled wheels.

French locomotive design, both in the days of the pre-nationalisation companies and following formation of the SNCF in 1938, was noteworthy for the reliance placed on compound-expansion locomotives, which despite their mechanical complexity—and hence need for skilled driving and careful maintenance—offered, size-for-size, performance and fuel economy unsurpassed throughout the world. Three mechanical engineers in particular brought compounding to a high degree of excellence, and the names of Vallantin of the PLM, Collin of the Nord, and Buchatel of the Est are as well known in France as are those of their contemporaries on this side of the Channel.

Greatest French railway engineer of all was André Chapelon, who revolutionised the theory and practice of locomotive steam generation and whose innovations in draughting arrangements, high superheat and internally-streamlined steam ports and passages were incorporated in engines designed throughout the world during and after the 1930's. It was as Chief Engineer of the Paris-Orléans Railway that Chapelon's name first attracted attention outside France; rebuilt P-O Pacifics turned out from Tours works in the early 1930's demonstrated the outstanding achievements made possible by incorporation of Chapelon principles, and soon more and more engineers were designing them into new locomotives, both compound and simple.

After nationalisation, as head of SNCF's Department of Steam Locomotive Studies, Chapelon devoted much of his attention to increasing locomotive efficiency by making the greatest possible use of every pound of steam. Some of his designs are described on the following pages; and but for the changed economic climate of the 1950's it seems certain that their successors, a range of standardised three-cylinder compounds which Chapelon formulated after the war, would have entered service in large numbers instead of remaining merely a set of blueprints. Designs for a 4-6-4, 4-8-4, 2-8-4 and 2-10-4 were evolved, but all were stillborn in the face of spreading electrification. If any one engine can be categorized as embodying all of Chapelon's ideals, it is his unique 242 A1 of 1946, a three-cylinder compound 4-8-4 that developed 4200 drawbar horsepower and on trial maintained a steady 62 mile/h up a grade of 1 in 155 with an 856t load. Though A1 remained the sole example of its class, Chapelon's Mountains, Mikados and Pacifics continued to excite the admiration of engineers and enthusiasts until the very end of French steam operation.

The 1930's saw the introduction of high-speed trains across the length and breadth of Europe. In Germany, 12 principal locomotive types were built during that decade; for express-passenger work, the handsome Pacifics of Class 01, with two cylinders, were followed by the four-cylinder compounds of Class 02. The 04 series were larger four-cylinder compounds carrying a high-pressure boiler working at 355lb/in²; and most successful of all were the 03 two-cylinder design, of which almost 300 were built, and their 03.10 class three-cylinder variant, of which 03.1082 is pictured at Cologne with an express for Frankfurt.

19

Heading a typical lightweight German passenger train of the mid-1950's is
Type 23 2-6-2 No. 23.050, a two-cylinder mixed-traffic locomotive introduced by the Bundesbahn in 1950 as a development of the Reichsbahn
Type 23 of 1940. 105 of the postwar engines were turned out, the first new
passenger locomotives to be built in Western Germany since the beginning
of the war, and ultimately the final steam power to remain in production.

Few European railways during the decade following World War 2 were without a fleet of the Reichsbahn two-cylinder 2-10-0s of Type 52—the wartime austerity freight locomotive of which almost 6,300 were built. Both plate-frame and bar-frame varieties were produced: 52.5052, one of the latter, rolls south over Austria's Sudbahn main line in May 1959.

Doyen of French steam locomotive engineers, André Chapelon, achieved worldwide renown in the early 1930's with his redesign of 20 Paris-Orleans Railway compound Pacifics of 1909; his innovations subsequently revolutionised European design practice. One of those super-Pacifics, as SNCF 231 E 4, is still in active mainline service here at Lille in 1961.

The massive DB 2-8-4T of Type 65 was introduced in 1951 to replace older German 2-8-2T designs in fast suburban-passenger operation. Most of the Type 65s were based on Darmstadt and Dusseldorf, where 65.015 stands ready for departure on an August evening in 1956.

Last and most outstanding of all French express locomotives was 232 U 1, a four-cylinder compound 4-6-4 that embodied all the experience of multi-cylinder engines, both simple and compound, gathered over the years. Based on the de Caso Hudsons introduced on the SNCF's Northern Region in 1939—the three-cylinder 232 R and four-cylinder 232 S classes—U 1 entered service in 1949 as a modified de Glehn compound with the high-pressure cylinders between the frames, Walschaerts valve gear replacing the Dabeg poppet valves of the earlier engines. Other refinements included a Standard three-jet stoker, feed-water heater, and roller bearings on all axles.

In operation, the locomotive started from rest as a four-cylinder simple and automatically changed over to compound working as speed increased; tractive effort in the latter form was 47,000lb, and 4000 ihp. was developed on test. 232 U 1 spent her entire life based at La Chapelle depot, Paris, working high-speed expresses north to Aulnoye and Lille; I photographed her during a footplate journey at the head of Train 171, the 12.05 pm Paris Nord to Aulnoye, in May 1959.

France was the first country in Europe to adopt the 4-8-2 type, similar designs appearing on both the Est and the PLM in 1925. Forty-one were built for the former railway by Fives-Lille, big de Glehn-du Bousquet four-cylinder compounds with *hand-fired* 48ft² grates. Most survived through the 1950's: 241 A 15 is alert at Nancy with a Paris express in 1959.

26

The PLM 4-8-2s mentioned on the previous page were to form the basis, 22 years later, for Chapelon's 241 P Mountains for the SNCF. 35 of these impressive four-cylinder compounds were turned out by Schneider at Le Creusot between 1947 and 1951; 241 P 29 leaves Lille for Paris shortly before the line was turned over to electric traction in June 1958.

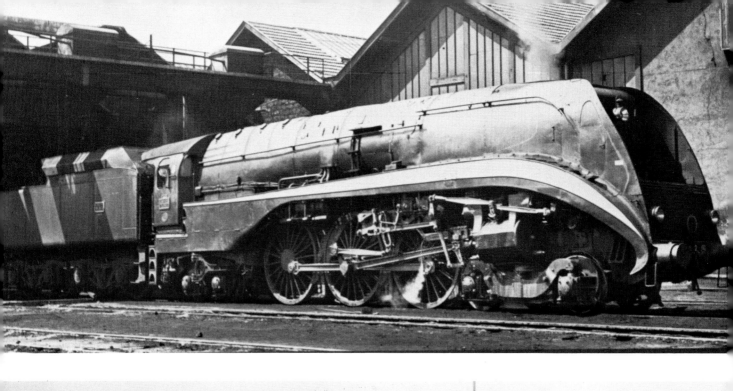

Four-cylinder compound version of the de Caso Hudson is represented by 232 S 2, one of four built in 1939-40 for working heavy expresses between Paris, Lille and the Belgian frontier.

◁

Stored out of service at Vitry is Chapelon's 160 A 1, a unique six-cylinder 2-12-0 compound completed in June 1940. Poppet valves and steam-jacketed cylinders aided efficiency; tractive power was 65,000lb. In store until 1948, 160 A 1 entered service too late to affect the trend to electrification, and was cut up seven years later.

Switzerland, though early to complete the electrification of its main lines, retained a number of steam engines for transfer-freight operation until 1965. Biggest and most powerful were the four-cylinder compound 2-10-0s of Class C5/6, 30 of which were produced by the Swiss Locomotive Co, Winterthur, for service over the Gotthard line during the first world war. Weighing 128 tonnes and developing 45,000lb tractive effort, the engines incorporated a Krauss-Helmholz leading truck and Heusinger valve gear. 2961, dating from 1915, was one of three shunting in the Basle freight yards on 12 May 1959.

The first 4-8-0s in Europe were introduced in 1915, forming the 570 class of Austria's Sudbahn. After the first world war and the formation of the kingdom of Austria, the principal traffic flow became east-west, rather than north-south, and the Vienna-Salzburg line of the newly-formed OBB received the majority of 40 similar 4-8-0s built between 1923 and 1928. Numbered 33.101-140 under the Reichsbahn régime, most survived World War 2. Fitted with Lentz valves and Giesl exhaust, 33.122 here heads a Rome-Vienna express at St. Veit, Carinthia, in 1959.

30

OBB 297.402, a 2-12-2T built in 1941, was one of the two most powerful rack-and-adhesion locomotives in Europe, producing some 52,000lb tractive effort and designed to haul 400t iron-ore trains over the 1 in 14 Abt rack sections of the Vordernberg-Eisenerz line in Styria. Sister engine 401 is preserved for museum display.

▷

Largest of the three German wartime freight-locomotive designs was the Reichsbahn Type 42 two-cylinder 2-10-0 of 1943. Some 900 were turned out, 338 of them at the Floridsdorf works, Vienna: 42.2513 is one of the latter, seen at Murzzuschlag, Styria, in the snows of February 1960.

Among the last passenger engines to see active service in Austria were the two-cylinder simple-expansion 2-6-2s of Class 35. Formerly Class 429 of the Austrian State Railway, engines of this design formed part of the stock of the Czech, Jugoslav and Italian Railways; 35.213, fitted with Giesl exhaust but otherwise in original condition, is one of about 20 of the class which until the early 1960's monopolised passenger service on the former Kronprinz Rudolf Bahn.

Both two-cylinder and three-cylinder versions of Dr. Lehner's big 2-8-4 passenger locomotive were tried out on the Vienna-Salzburg main line: the choice ultimately fell on the former, 13 of which were built for the OBB and could be found until the mid-1950's handling the heaviest passenger trains over the Semmering route of the Sudbahn. Lentz oscillating-cam poppet valves and 6ft 4in coupled wheels gave them a speed on trials of 96 mile/h; tractive effort was 44,000lb. 12.03 (lower) is of the 1931 batch; 12.12 represents the modified 1936 version.

Austrian version of the D.R. Type 52: fitted with Giesl exhaust and carrying a guard's cabin aboard the tender, 2.3316 is heading a southbound freight over the Semmering Pass in 1961.

...argest and most influential railway in Europe, the Prussian ...tate dominated locomotive design for a quarter of a century. ...ven after formation of the Reichsbahn in 1920, Prussian ...esigns were perpetuated, and many of them remained in ...ervice throughout Europe until the very end of steam. ...uperpower of its era, Prussian G-10 0-10-0 No. 657.3268 is ...ne of almost 80 still in use on the ÖBB in 1960.

The locomotives of Holland have remained relatively little-known to British travellers, though many of them were of importance in the overall development of European steam power. The 6301 class four-cylinder 4-8-4 tanks, for example, were the most powerful tank engines in Europe at the time of their introduction in 1931: they handled much of the heavy coal and mineral traffic of South Limburg. After World War 2, two new three-cylinder designs were introduced: 15 4-6-0s and 35 0-8-0s built in Sweden. One of the latter, NoHAB-built 0-8-0 4709, shunts the freight yard at Maastricht in June 1957.

Neighbours at the Milan Smistamento roundhouse in May 1964 are two-cylinder 2-8-0 No. 735.313 and, at rear, four-cylinder 2-6-2 No. 685.626.

Italian State Railways four-cylinder simple Pacific 691.012 at Venice Santa Lucia in May 1959. Italy's most powerful freight design (below) is represented by 2-10-0 No. 480.007 at Milan.

Construction of steam locomotives for Italy's State Railways ceased in 1930; several noteworthy developments, nonetheless, were introduced in Italy and widely adopted elsewhere, such as Caprotti valve gear, the Zara leading truck (combining the radial wheels and leading coupled wheels in one bogie) and the Franco-Crosti boiler. 735.313, photographed in Milan in 1959, is one of several hundred two-cylinder 2-8-0s dating from 1917.

38

Most widely-used express-passenger locomotives in Italy were the four-cylinder simple 2-6-2s of Class 685; similar compound engines of three classes (680, 681 and 682) were rebuilt as simples, many of them subsequently being modified with Caprotti valve gear. One of these, 685.634, here heads the 7.22 am Venice-Vienna express at Udine on 6 May 1959.

For many years the Belgian National Railways relied on the famous Flamme Pacifics for haulage of its heaviest main-line expresses. In 1935, in readiness for a general increase in speed of its passenger services, the SNCB took delivery of 15 heavy four-cylinder Pacifics that packed great power into a compact size. To assist in hand-firing the 54ft² grate, two firedoors were provided; outside Walschaerts valve gear operated the inside valves through rocking shafts, and compressed-air sanding gear fed the 6ft 6in coupled wheels.

In operation, these Class 1 Pacifics proved capable of hauling with ease 700-ton trains over the 71-mile Ostend-Brussels main line in 60 minutes. By 1938 a total of 35 were in service; during the German occupation, only their very high axle loading of 23½ tons prevented their being taken to Germany as 'prizes of war'. The 1950's saw many of the class again handling heavy trains over the remaining non-electrified routes radiating from the capital, and this photograph of 1.027 shows her in June 1958 shortly before leaving Brussels Midi with a passenger train for the French frontier

The heavy Pacifics described on the previous page handled all but the fastest Belgian passenger trains. In May 1938 the SNCB inaugurated an ultra-high speed lightweight train service twice daily between Brussels and Ostend, on a record-breaking schedule that included a start-to-stop timing of 46 minutes for the 57.7 miles from Brussels to Bruges; to work it they introduced six inside-cylinder Atlantics, four with Walschaerts valve gear and two with poppet valves. Driving wheels were 6ft 10⅝in in diameter. 12.001, first of the class, is pictured at Lille in northern France; 12.004 has been preserved for museum display.

Predecessor of the two Belgian express engines just described, yet still in service alongside them in 1958, was 10.018, last of the legendary four-cylinder Pacifics designed by J. B. Flamme and introduced between 1910 and 1914. The inside cylinders drove the leading coupled axle; to enable the rear axle to clear the very large firebox, they were carried in a lengthy extension of the frames ahead of the leading bogie, giving the engines the unique appearance shown here. 58 were built, and in their final form—including larger superheater, double blastpipe and chimney, and ACFI feedwater heater—they were among the most notable engines of their era.

43

EASTERN EUROPE: steam's final flowering

The Soviet bloc countries and the USSR itself, certainly into the early 1970's, still displayed some unique features of locomotive design: unhindered by the western world's rapid approach to complete dieselisation, steam locomotive development continued in Russia, Poland and Czechoslovakia for many years after it had effectively ceased on most Western European and North American railways, and even today much freight traffic, in particular, is steam-powered throughout Eastern Europe.

Russian locomotive engineers borrowed heavily from American practice in developing their own brand of superpower. Most widely distributed today, and the first design to take advantage of the twenty-ton axle loading made possible in the mid-1930's, were the FD class 2-10-2s, of which more than 3,000 were built; both these and their passenger counterparts, the IS (Iosif Stalin) class 2-8-4s of 1932, incorporate bar frames, mechanical stokers and thermic syphons. Experimental locomotives of the period included a unique and shortlived 4-14-4, three high-speed streamlined Hudsons and, with a tractive effort of 89,300lb, the most powerful Beyer-Garratt ever built.

Postwar Soviet designs were predominantly standardised freight locomotives. More noteworthy were the superb P36 class 4-8-4s illustrated on page 49, and two simple-articulated 2-8-8-4s built at Kolomna in 1954.

Czechoslovakia, where steam power continued in production until 1957, developed four impressive postwar designs of 4-8-2, in both two- and three-cylinder versions; and the two-cylinder 556 class of heavy freight 2-10-0, of which 510 were built between 1952 and 1957. The most advanced tank engines built in Europe were also Czech, the 22 three-cylinder 4-8-4 tanks of Class 477, introduced in 1955. In all respects save coal and water capacity, these paralleled their tender-engine counterparts, incorporating thermic syphons, Kylchap exhausts, mechanical stokers and roller bearings on all axles. Neighbouring Poland, too, boasted a superpower tank engine, the Okz-32 class of 2-10-2T; 25 were built in 1934-36 and many were still handling express-passenger trains in the late 1960's. Postwar 2-10-0s included 100 ALCO, Baldwin and Lima imports and, derived from them in the final flowering of Polish steam design, the Ty-51 class of 232 big and handsome freight locomotives still active on every Polish main line today.

Romanian superpower: CFR two-cylinder 2-8-4 No. 142.072 is one of 79 built at Malaxa and Resita between 1937-1940. Based on the Austrian design pictured on page 32, the CFR engines were still active well into the 1970's: three others were in steam here at Timisoara as 072 backed down to her train on 22 May 1971.

Poland's principal express-passenger type, apart from a class of three relatively unsuccessful 4-8-2s, was the Pt-31 class two-cylinder 2-8-2 designed at the Chrzanow works in 1932. 110 were built between then and 1940, the last 12 as Deutsche Reichsbahn Nos. 39. 1001-12, and a further 180 produced after the war were slightly modernised and classed Pt-47. Many of the latter are still active today—unlike the Pt-31 seen here soon after withdrawal in 1960.

Still vigorously developing steam power for a decade after the war, Czechoslovakian locomotive engineers produced some of Europe's most advanced and impressive designs. Four varieties of 4-8-2 were among them; 475.139, photographed at Brno on a local passenger train in September 1971, is a two-cylinder mixed traffic engine with a taper boiler incorporating thermic syphons, and with roller bearings throughout. 140 were built, followed by five similar three-cylinder compounds.

Previous pages (21 and 31) have illustrated the Deutsche Reichsbahn 52 and 42 classes of wartime freight locomotives. Forerunner of both was the Type 50 of 1938, a powerful two-cylinder 2-10-0 with bar frames of which almost 2200 were produced. A compliment to their advanced design is here evident in CFR 150.158, a Romanian version of the DR Type 50 built at Resita in 1957 and still at work in 1975.

For many years under the Soviet régime, freight traffic in the USSR had priority, and passenger travel was limited by a strict system of permits and controls. For ten years after the war no passenger locomotives were constructed, other than a single prototype 4-8-4. In 1954, however, construction of this type, the P36, began to such effect that in two years some 250 were in service. All built at Kolomna, the P36s had 6ft 1in coupled wheels, 213lb boiler pressure and a 73ft² grate: they developed 2500 dbhp. Many remained in service in Siberia as recently as mid-1974.

J. N. Westwood

IBERIA: selection and rationalisation

South of the Pyrenees there accumulated examples of almost every school of locomotive design; the railways of Spain alone boasted the products of more than 50 European builders, plus those of ALCO and Baldwin in the United States. Longevity was a keynote of many of the engines built for the four major companies—Norte, Andaluces, Oeste and Madrid, Zaragoza & Alicante Railways—which were merged in 1941 to form the RENFE, and as late as 1961 I photographed in Valencia, side-by-side and in steam, a year-old Beyer-Garratt and an 0-6-0 built by C. B. Wilson of Leeds in 1857.

In Spain, as in Russia, strategic considerations dictated a rail gauge of 1.67m (about 5ft 6in); in the later years of steam locomotive development, as a typically Spanish school of design began to supplement that imported prior to about 1920, this helped give indigenous steam power a uniquely broad and massive appearance. Five Spanish firms constructed the majority of the country's standard-gauge steam power from that time on: Macosa and Construcciones Devis of Valencia, Babcock & Wilcox and Euskalduna in Bilbao, and Maquinista Terrestre y Maritima (MTM) in Barcelona. All five produced what became the principal main-line type on the pregrouping systems—large mixed-traffic 4-8-0s of which 505 were ultimately turned out, almost all remaining in service well into the 1960's. Most were two-cylinder, simple-expansion machines, only the Norte perpetuating in these more modern designs the de Glehn system of compounding which had characterised its earlier imports.

As increasing train loads demanded ever more powerful engines, the Norte again led the way to compound 4-8-2s, introducing in 1925 the first of a series of four-cylinder compounds which ultimately totalled 66 engines. One of them, 241.4048, was rebuilt with Dabeg poppet valves, and this version was chosen for postwar construction by the RENFE, 28 almost identical locomotives entering service in 1946-48 on the former Norte main line between Avila and the French frontier at Irun: until electrification of much of the Norte network, these remained among the most impressive locomotives in Spain. Some notable simple-expansion Mountains, contemporary with the Norte compounds, were put into service by the MZA during the 1920s and 1930s, 95 of them of conventional appearance and the final ten streamlined in the fashion of the Belgian Pacific illustrated on pages 40-41. Maximum speeds on even the fastest Spanish steam-hauled expresses hardly warranted streamlining, and the ten engines led a mundane career on the MZA, then Oueste, and finally Norte passenger services. Final development of the Spanish 4-8-2 was a series of 57 two-cylinder giants, tipping the scales at 202t, built by RENFE for the MZA lines from Madrid to Alicante and to Seville.

Sharing the same design of boiler as these culminating 4-8-2s were 22 equally-impressive 2-10-2s, introduced between 1942-45 to work heavy coal traffic out of the Ponferrada coalfields. Most powerful non-articulated locomotives in Europe, these massive three-cylinder machines produced a tractive effort of 72,050lb and incorporated such refinements as feed-water heaters and electric lighting. One of them is shown opposite on an autumn morning in 1959: stoker-fired 151.3112 accelerating a 70-wagon RENFE freight out of Leon for Venta de Banos.

The final step in Spanish steam evolution was the introduction in 1955 of ten superb 4-8-4s, built by MTM for main-line express work between Avila and Alsasua, the then unelectrified section of the former Norte line to France. Painted green and impeccably maintained, these big Northerns exemplified the best in Iberian locomotive design.

Portugal, with similar mountainous territory to that in Spain, but with appreciably lighter rail traffic, relied primarily on French and German imports for its broad-gauge system. Many were de Glehn compounds, including 4-6-0s and Pacifics for the Minho-Douro and South Eastern State Railways and three powerful four-cylinder 4-8-0s supplied by Henschel in 1930 for the Beira Alta, a privately-owned railway linking the Lisbon-Porto main line at Pamphilhosa with the Spanish system at Vilar Formoso. Further 4-8-0s were built by Devis, MTM and Babcock & Wilcox—Spain's only exported locomotives—for the South Eastern State Railway in 1947; the only other postwar steam locomotives were 22 ALCO 2-8-2s put into service in 1944-45.

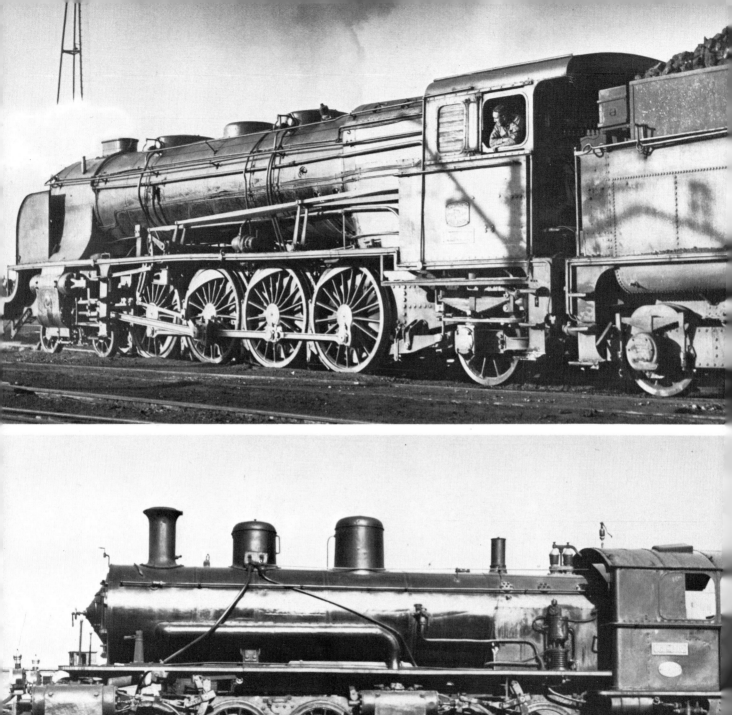

First 4-8-2s to see service in Spain were four-cylinder compounds introduced on the Norte in 1925. Several varieties followed, and the type was perpetuated by the RENFE between 1946-1948. One of a batch built by Euskalduna in 1927, 241. 4010 prepares to leave León for Palencia in October 1957.

◁

Broad-gauge Mallet compounds were rare indeed: 060.4002, still active on the steeply-graded Valencia-Utiel line in 1964, was one of nine built by Henschel for the Central of Aragon between 1912 and 1928. Similar 2-6-6-0 compounds were retired in the 1950's.

Another type exclusive to the Norte, ALCO-built 2-8-2s, proved a useful mixed-traffic machine for Spanish conditions, and after formation of the RENFE in 1943 a total of 242 big two-cylinder Mikados were turned out by the four major Spanish builders and by North British in Glasgow. 141F.2368, here accelerating a northbound express out of Alicante, is an oil-burner built by Babcock & Wilcox in 1956. Construction continued until 1960, and throughout the next decade the class handled trains of all types with reliability and economy; several of the newer locomotives remain in service today.

On an October afternoon in 1957, 242F.2003 moves the southbound 13-coach 'Iberia Express' out of Valladolid. Most impressive of all RENFE passenger engines, ten of these oil-burning 4-8-4s were built in 1955-56 to handle increasingly heavy trains over the non-electrified sections of the Madrid-Irun main line. With two 25 × 28in cylinders, 6ft 3in coupled wheels and 228lb boiler pressure, design tractive effort was 46,900lb; Lentz poppet valves were actuated by Walschaerts gear.

Europe's most powerful non-articulated locomotives, 22 massive three-cylinder 2-10-2s were put into service between 1942-1945 to handle heavy coal trains from the Ponferrada coalfields to the north-coast port of La Coruna. Tractive force was 72,050lb; seven of the class were oil-burners, two others fitted with mechanical stokers. Here 151.3107 nears León, Castile, with an evening freight from Palencia.

55

The steeply-graded main line of the former Central of Aragon between Valencia and Teruel climbs for nine miles at a gradient of 1 in 46, and to work this route six Pacific Garratts were built in 1930 by Euskalduna, Bilbao. These 4-6-2 + 2-6-4 oil-burners were equipped with le Chatelier counter-pressure brakes for safety on the steep descents, and had coupled wheels no less than 5ft 9in in diameter, a figure exceeded only by the 5ft 11in Pacific Garratts built in 1936 for the Constantine-Oran main line in Algeria.

Numbered 462F.0401 to 0406, the entire class was transferred in 1959 to the old Northern line out of Valencia, to help improve timekeeping of the heavy Seville-Barcelona through trains. At the head of one of these, 462F.0401 pauses to take water at Benicarlo in September 1961.

57

Barreiro terminal, on the south side of the Tagus opposite Lisbon, was springboard of Portugal's South Eastern State Railway. Ready for their trains on 27 May 1965 are former South Eastern compound Pacific No. 552 and the same railway's two-cylinder freight 2-8-0 No. 707.

Majesty of Spanish steam: a four-cylinder compound 4-8-2 greets the sun at Valladolid, on the former Norte main line for which she was built in 1930. The Babcock & Wilcox plant in Bilbao was her birthplace.

59

AFRICA: Kingdom of the Beyer-Garratt

Evolution of the articulated locomotive, which in its infancy took one of several basic forms, ultimately followed three paths—the Beyer-Garratt, the Mallet compound, and the latter's derivative, the simple articulated which was to represent the final phase of steam locomotive development in North America.

Where the steep, but generally well-aligned and heavily-ballasted railroads of that continent favoured the Mallet form of articulation, elsewhere in the world—and particularly in Africa—railways had often been laid with sharp curves and to narrow track gauges. On them the Mallet, with its boiler placed conventionally above the wheels, became increasingly impractical as heavier loads demanded higher steaming capacity; the Garratt boiler, with its barrel slung between the two engine units, could be of greater diameter while still meeting the limits of a restrictive loading gauge. The Garratt form of articulation, similarly, was better suited to sharply-curving, lightly-laid track than was the more rigid Mallet.

Even in Africa, the Mallet had its day: the biggest tender-engine ever to run on the 3ft 6in gauge was a North British-built 2-6-6-2 Mallet compound designed for freight service on the steeply-graded Natal main line between Durban and Cato Ridge. The leading, low-pressure cylinders were no less than 31½in in diameter, helping produce a tractive force of some 65,000lb. That design, however, represented the swan song of the Mallet in South Africa, and indeed throughout the British Commonwealth: in 1921 one of the class was extensively tested against a 2-6-6-2 Beyer-Garratt, and proved no match in terms of economy, haulage capacity or speed. From that time on, the Garratt became the standard, all-purpose articulated locomotive in South Africa, Rhodesia and East Africa, and on the Luanda and Benguela railways on the west coast. Further north, the world's first 4-6-4 + 4-6-4 Garratts were delivered to the Sudan railways, and in Algeria twelve Pacific Garratts delivered by Société Franco-Belge in 1936 were true express-passenger engines, one of them successfully handling Calais-Paris boat expresses before being shipped from France, and another achieving 82 mile/h on trials in Algeria after delivery.

South of the equator, Kenya's Mombasa-Nairobi main line saw introduction of the first 4-8-4 + 4-8-4 type, the EC3 class of 1939, and of the 59 class 4-8-2 + 2-8-4s of 1955. 34 of the latter were built, largest and most powerful locomotives ever to run on the metre gauge; weighing 252 tons and developing 83,350lb of tractive effort, they have for twenty years monopolised heavy freight traffic between the coast and Kenya's mile-high capital.

Rhodesia, too, developed a family of Garratts with which to handle virtually all its main-line traffic, both passenger and freight, and a total of 250 were delivered between 1926 and 1958. Best-known are the 4-6-4 + 4-6-4s of Class 15, mixed-traffic machines with streamlined tanks fore and aft, which for many years worked all the through trains over the 484-mile line between Bulawayo and the South African city of Mafeking. For purely freight work, the 15s were supplemented by massive stoker-fired Class 20 4-8-2 + 2-8-4s, developing 69,330lb of tractive effort. 61 of these were delivered between 1954-58; many worked the heavy coal and ore traffic between Wankie and the Copper Belt of what is now Zambia, 44 of the class passing to the Zambian Railways upon that country's independence in 1967.

In South Africa, of more than 400 Garratts delivered since 1921 some 370 are in service today, the largest concentration of such machines anywhere. Tipping the scales in weight and power are the six remaining 4-8-2 + 2-8-4s of Class GL, described on page 63. After 40 years handling coal trains between Vryheid and Glencoe, a line now electrified, the GLs today share in the work of their more modern GMA and GO class sisters. Most modern of all South Africa's Garratts are the 2ft gauge 2-6-2 + 2-6-2s built by Hunslet Taylor in 1968, the last of a line of narrow-gauge superpower well represented by the photograph (opposite) of 126 at Umzinto, eastern terminal of Natal's branch from Donnybrook to the Indian Ocean. With them, perhaps, the evolution of H. W. Garratt's patent 2ft gauge locomotive of 60 years earlier, that in the intervening years helped change the face of Africa, has come full circle.

World's most powerful non-articulated engines on the 3ft 6in gauge, and the final main-line steam power in South Africa, are the massive Class 25 4-8-4s, fifty of which were built by North British and Henschel in 1952-54. Ninety similar engines were fitted with condensing equipment: exhaust steam from the cylinders returns to the tender, an exhaust fan in the smokebox providing the draught for combustion.

The two classes monopolise Cape Northern services between Kimberley, de Aar and Beaufort West; Henschel-built 3424 heads a northbound express in January 1967.

Lead engine of Beyer-Garratt 4097 at Krugersdorp, Transvaal, emphasises the power and size of these Cape-gauge giants. Biggest of all SAR locomotives are seven 4-8-2 + 2-8-4 stoker-fired Garratts of Class GL, weighing 214 tons and developing 90,000lb tractive force; 4097 represents a 1956 version of the same wheel arrangement, designed for 60lb rail and developing 68,800lb tractive effort within a weight of 189 tons.

Far from the erecting halls of Schenectady, SAR Class 15CA No. 2042 at the head of this Witbank-Pretoria oil train is one of 23 Mountains delivered by ALCO in 1926, when South African Railways made their first comparative trials of modern North American motive power. Other 4-8-2s to the same design came from Baldwin, Breda and North British, ultimately totalling 96 locomotives: most remain in service today. Rear engine, adding its 37,000lb tractive effort to the 48,000lb of 2042, is an unrebuilt Hendrie 4-8-2 of Class 15A.

Bloemfontein, railway crossroads of South Africa, is the goal of Class 15F 4-8-2 No. 3069 heading east over the Orange Free State main line with freight from Kimberley. Originally introduced in 1938, several batches of almost identical locomotives were built, until by 1948 a total of 255 had entered service. 3069 is one of the final batch, North British-built with mechanical stoker, Walschaerts valve gear and a double-bogie tender.

Nowhere in the world has the 4-8-2 wheel arrangement been developed so extensively: in the late 1960's some 1300 of the type were in use on South Africa's railways.

Express-passenger power of the former Cape Government Railway was Beatty's Class 4 4-8-2, with bar frames and inside Stephenson valve gear. Developed into Class 4AR, and here represented by 1556 at Krugersdorp, the type received a larger, standard boiler and Walschaerts gear: note the uncommon leading eccentric rod, actuating outside-admission valves. Ten were built by North British, and all remained in service as late as 1973.

First and only 'home-made' engines in South Africa were ten SI class 0-8-0 shunters, turned out from Salt River works, Cape Town, in 1947. 25 further members of the class, including 3815 pictured here at Germiston, followed in 1954. The locomotives pack 43,000lb of tractive effort into their compact size: cylinders are 23 × 25in, coupled wheels 4ft in diameter, and engine weight 74½ tons.

Trailing an auxiliary water tank, Beyer-Garratt 4110 heads north beneath the catenary spanning the main line near Faure, Cape Province. Paarden Eiland motive power depot, Cape Town, houses Garratts of two classes, the GEA 4-8-2 + 2-8-4s built by Beyer Peacock in 1945-47, and the later GMAs of the same type, built by both British and German firms during the 1950's. 4110 emerged from the North British erecting shops in Glasgow in 1957.

Four cylinders and sixteen coupled wheels develop every ounce of their rated 69,000lb tractive force as GMAM Garratt 4116 battles up the tortuous 1 in 40 approach to Sir Lowry's Pass, on the Cape Province branch to Caledon and Bredasdorp. Escarpment of the Hottentot Holland range looms in the background; the train here makes almost a full circle in its nine-mile climb towards the plateau.

69

The 4-8-4 was North America's favourite wheel arrangement in the last quarter-century of steam: close to 1000 were built between Northern Pacific's 2600 of 1926 and Reading Company's 2102 of 1945. The Reading-built Mountain here rolls out of Gettysburg on the road's freight-only branch to Mount Holly Springs.

NORTH AMERICA: from Triplex to 'Big Boy'

No country had greater influence on worldwide trends in locomotive design than the United States. More than 100,000 steam locomotives were built there between 1900 and 1950, some 37,000 of them for export; characteristics common to all were ruggedness, reliability, ease of maintenance, and abundant power output with little concern for fuel consumption.

Historically, the American steam locomotive opened up the country to a far greater extent than in Europe. Elsewhere than in the early-settled areas of the eastern seaboard, the railroad generally preceded industry and habitation and hence was relatively free of restrictions on gauge: rolling stock could reach a width of eleven feet and a height of sixteen, and on many western roads even these generous dimensions could be exceeded. Long, single-track lines with infrequent sidings were the rule, and in turn trains were appreciably heavier than their overseas counterparts. Since few roads manufactured their own rolling stock the majority of technical advances were made by the three principal locomotive builders—Baldwin, Lima and the American Locomotive Company.

Starting power and steaming capacity largely dictated locomotive design, and by the mid-1920's all three builders could claim some remarkable achievements. ALCO had built the first Mallet compound in 1904, and the type blossomed into 2-6-6-2, 4-4-6-2, 2-8-8-2 and even 2-10-10-2 form; Baldwin engineer George R. Henderson took the concept to its ultimate in designing a six-cylinder triple-articulated 2-8-8-8-2 for the Erie— the *Matt Shay* and two similar engines built in 1916— and a stillborn quadruplex 2-8-8-8-8-2 for Santa Fe. More practically, ALCO espoused the three-cylinder simple-expansion design, of which the most noteworthy were the 88 big 4-12-2s of 1926 that successfully hauled Union Pacific freight for the next 30 years; and the high-pressure concept fathered by Delaware & Hudson president L. F. Loree, represented on that road by three cross-compound 2-8-0s and the unique triple-expansion 4-8-0 *L. F. Loree* of 1930.

The Lima Locomotive Corporation, meanwhile, was developing conventional high-power designs from the drawing-board of W. E. Woodard, and in 1925 there emerged the first truly modern superpower locomotive, Lima's demonstrator A-1: the first American 2-8-4 and the engine that more than any other influenced the final quarter-century of US steam locomotive design. The trailing truck permitted a huge firebox: its 100ft² grate was unmatched by any other non-articulated engine, boiler pressure was 240lb/in², and tractive force some 72,000lb. Ultimately more than 600 Berkshires took to North American rails, including the very last locomotives built by both Lima and ALCO 25 years later. 'Super power' was virtually a Lima trademark: Will Woodard's next notable design was a 2-10-4, and this, too, matched the railroads' growing demands for horsepower and steaming capacity at high speeds.

Final vindication of the superpower concept, perhaps, was the 4-8-4, destined to become North America's favourite wheel arrangement in the last decades of steam: legendary among 4-8-4s are the 60 Lima-built Southern Pacific streamliners; one of them, 4459, ran her first million miles in less than eight years' service, while sister-engine 4449 is currently steaming through 1976 at the head of the bicentennial 'American Freedom Train'.

US freight superpower is typified by the simple-articulated locomotives, developed from the true Mallet compounds, that saw out the final years of steam operation. For a decade after their introduction in 1928 the Northern Pacific Z5 2-8-8-4s were the world's biggest: tractive force was 140,000lb and their 182ft² grate was never exceeded. High speeds were commonplace with some, such as Union Pacific's 'Challenger' 4-6-6-4s that were equally at home on freight or express passenger workings; others, like Chesapeake & Ohio's H8 2-6-6-6s, spent their lives on heavy coal drags. And as late as 1958 the greatest of them all, Union Pacific's 540-ton 'Big Boy' 4-8-8-4s, were still in operation to typify the ultimate in North American steam.

Union Pacific's brief to the American Locomotive Company was specific: 'Build us the biggest locomotive possible within our loading gauge; design it to move 3,600-ton trains up 1 in 90 grades without a helper; and build it to run safely at 80 miles per hour'.

The result was the legendary 'Big Boy', a simple-articulated 4-8-8-4 that could out-pull at speed any locomotive built, before or since. Twenty were turned out from ALCO's Schenectady plant in 1941, five more in 1944. Everything about them helped justify that epithet: 132ft 10in from coupler to coupler, turning the scales at 540 tons, and with one of the biggest fireboxes—150ft^2 of grate area—ever put on a locomotive. Boiler pressure was 300lb/in^2, coupled wheels 5ft 8in in diameter, and tractive effort 135,400lb. Once on the road, the engines performed even better than the specification demanded: they could roll 4,200-ton trains up the long 1 in 90 grades of the Wasatch mountains at a steady 20 mile/h, and on dynamometer-car test 4016 recorded a drawbar horsepower of 6290. Coal and water consumption at that level of power was similarly in keeping—22 tons of coal and 10,000 gallons of water hourly. Reliability was unquestioned, and for most of their lives the 'Big Boys' averaged a monthly 7,500 miles in revenue service.

Until the mid-1950's they reigned supreme between the UP's division points of Cheyenne and Laramie. In the summer of 1957, Sherman Hill and the UP main line west increasingly echoed to the sound of General Electric's new gas turbines. 1958 saw just 10 Big Boys in steam; and at the end of September of that year their fires were dropped for the last time.

72

Two Reading Railway
4-8-4s fight their way up
the 1 in 80 to Locust Gap
summit, between
Shamokin and
Tamaqua,
Pennsylvania.

Rigid-framed duplex drive was a keynote of Pennsylvania Railroad practice during the early 1940's. For freight service a solitary 4-6-4-4 was followed by 26 successful 4-4-6-4s; and for high-speed passenger work there came the magnificent TI 4-4-4-4, the last truly high-speed steam locomotive designed in North America. 52 were built: on expresses from Harrisburg to Chicago, 713 miles, they needed only one coaling stop, and regularly exceeded 100 mile/h with 1200-ton trains.

In original form, poppet-valved 6111 here heads the westbound 'Manhattan Limited' round Horseshoe Curve; subsequently, to aid maintenance, skirting was raised and shark-nose redesigned.

Few North American Pacifics, even, could outperform the big Pennsylvania 4-6-0s of Class G5s: they packed a 41,300lb tractive effort and were unsurpassed in heavy commuter service. The road's Juniata shops turned out 121 of the class.

Two distinctive express-passenger designs were Canadian Pacific's F1a 'Jubilee' class 4-4-4s, of which the last, No. 2929 of 1938, is in the foreground; and the Boston & Maine P4a Pacifics, represented by 3713. Lima built ten of the class in 1934 and 1937.

West End of Baltimore & Ohio Railroad's Cumberland Division—100 miles of sawtooth, 1 in 50 grades over the Alleghenies—was the battleground for B&O's EM-1 articulateds—30 Baldwin-built 2-8-8-4s delivered in 1944-45. Second of the class, 7601 approaches Altamont as she puts her 115,000lb of tractive force into the westbound ascent of Seventeen Mile Grade.

Final phase of Lima's superpower theme, the fast and powerful 2-8-4, is represented by Class S-2 759 of the NYCStL—the Nickel Plate Road. 65 were built between 1941 and 1949; almost identical machines were supplied to Chesapeake & Ohio, Louisville & Nashville, and Père Marquette.

SOUTH AMERICA: extremes of gauge and grade

A continent as vast as South America, spanning some 4400 miles in length and 3000 in breadth, and incorporating more than a dozen countries, not surprisingly shows little consistency in the operating practices of its many individual railways, nor in the locomotives that run on them. As in the Iberian peninsula, South American steam power displayed the practices of many European and North American builders; unlike Spain, however, no indigenous locomotive industry developed, and to the end of steam operation even the biggest and most modern locomotives bore such works plates as Baldwin and Henschel, Vulcan and Mitsubishi.

Argentina's railways were predominantly British-built and owned. Their motive power reflected this, and included examples of the most up-to-date designs offered by Britain's locomotive manufacturers. The Buenos Aires Great Southern, for example, operated some advanced three-cylinder Vulcan Pacifics, with 6ft 6in coupled wheels and a tractive effort of 30,700lb. The same builder supplied in the 1930's one of the final examples of two-cylinder cross-compounds built anywhere in the world, a class of twenty 2-8-2s for the Central Argentine Railway. Some of the biggest 2-8-2s in the continent, 205t engines for the 5ft 6in-gauge Buenos Aires Pacific Railway, were supplied by Beyer Peacock in 1928; their tractive effort was a rated 40,300lb. A less common wheel arrangement, the 4-8-0, was represented in Argentina by two classes designed by Vulcan in 1938 and 1948 respectively. Eight of the former, Class 15A, and 30 of the very similar Class 15B were imported, and many remained active into the 1970's on the South West Region (ex-General Roca, ex-BAGS) of the state-owned Argentine Railways. So, too, did the majority of an earlier design of 4-8-0, the three-cylinder 11C class, of which 75 were extensively rebuilt in 1958-59 to the designs of André Chapelon.

The last new steam locomotives, other than narrow-gauge types, to be built for the Argentine were 15 Henschel 2-10-0s delivered in 1952 to the then General Urquiza Railway, which comprised the 4ft 8½in-gauge lines in the north-east of the country. Their design closely followed that of five 2-10-0s supplied by the same builder to the state-owned railways of Uruguay two years earlier. Even later, the world's southernmost railway—the 75cm-gauge Rio Turbio, 1600 miles south of Buenos Aires—took delivery of two classes of heavy and powerful 2-10-2 freight engines to handle its coal traffic down to the coast at Rio Gallegos: both came from Mitsubishi in Japan, ten in 1956 and a final ten in 1963.

All of the railways mentioned traverse flat, open terrain and the need for true superpower locomotives was never as marked in the eastern part of the continent as it was on the mountain-climbing lines in the west. The railways of Colombia, Bolivia and Chile, for example, penetrate deep into the Andes on the metre or 3ft gauge, and both rack- and adhesion-worked lines have always demanded the most powerful locomotives. Among them were a variety of Kitson-Meyer type articulated engines: 0-6-8-0 and 0-8-6-0 rack-and-adhesion locomotives built in 1908 for the then Chilean Transandine Railway were still intact, though inactive, in 1969, and an exceptionally powerful representative of the type was a 2-8-8-2 built for the 3ft-gauge Colombian railways by Robert Stephenson & Co. in 1935. With 205lb boiler pressure and four 17¾ × 20in cylinders, the designed tractive effort was no less than 58,560lb, and on test the locomotive accelerated a 330t train from rest to 10 mile/h on a 1 in 22 grade. More conventional motive power entered service in Colombia in the late 1940's, in the form of rugged 4-8-2s supplied by Baldwin and H. K. Porter, and in the 1950's with some powerful 2-8-2s from the Belgian builder Tubize. One of the former, Baldwin-built Mountain 107, is shown opposite storming out of Bogotá with a mixed train in October 1967.

Largely North American practice was the keynote of the railways of Mexico, and as late as 1968 the main line north from Mexico City echoed to the exhaust of modern 4-8-4s outshopped from ALCO and Baldwin in 1946. Typifying the best in US steam design, the big Northerns were a magnet for enthusiasts long after withdrawal of their counterparts north of the border.

No mistaking ownership of this ALCO 4-8-4: Nacionales de
Mexico 3030 rouses the echoes of Valle de Mexico in March
1967 as she accelerates north with a 65-car freight for San Juan
del Rio. ALCO and Baldwin produced 32 of the big Northerns
in 1946; a dozen were still active when this picture was made.

First railway to link Mexico City with the east-coast port of Vera Cruz was the British-built Ferrocarril Mexicano. Though taken over by the NdeM in 1946, FCM locomotives retained their distinctive livery and lettering until the end of steam in the late 1960's; Mexicano 218 is one of ten Baldwin-built 2-8-0s of 1946, patterned after the 'Pershing' locomotives exported to Europe during the second world war.

A Baldwin export of 1944 was Ferrocarriles de Colombia 4-8-2 No. 107, still in active service in Bogotá in October 1967. Though constructed to 3ft gauge, the Colombian railways traverse mountainous country and their steam power was rugged and reliable.

Four thousand miles to the south, another No. 107 rolls west out of Rio Gallegos, seaport terminal of the world's southernmost railway. The big 2-10-2 is one of ten supplied to the 160-mile Ramal Ferroviario Industrial Rio Turbio by Mitsubishi in 1956.

Both Uruguay and Argentina bought big steam power in the 1950's: Henschel 2-10-0s for standard-gauge operation, five for Uruguay and 15 for the General Urquiza Railway in Argentina. One of the latter, 3002 of 1952, glistens in the evening sun at Basavilbaso in July 1969.

photographs: M. H. J. Finch

SOUTH PACIFIC: Australian and New Zealand steam

Australia's railways were developed primarily to serve the major cities of the southeast—Sydney, Melbourne, Adelaide and Brisbane. Each state was fiercely competitive towards its neighbours, and one result was the lack of agreement on a standardised track gauge: New South Wales alone remains a stronghold of 4ft 8½in operation, surrounded by the 5ft 3in of Victoria and South Australia and the 3ft 6in of the latter state and of Queensland.

Motive-power development, similarly, reflected this autonomy. From the 1920's on, following the appointment of Missouri-Kansas-Texas engineer W. A. Webb as Commissioner of Railways, South Australia hewed closely to American practice; hallmark of the Webb regime was the fleet of US-styled steam power that took the rails between 1926 and the second World War. Ten big 4-8-2s of Class 500, later converted to booster-fitted 4-8-4s, took over principal SAR freight services, and 6ft 3in-drivered Pacifics set the pace for the main-line expresses. In 1930 came Australia's only 2-8-4s, booster-fitted freight engines that developed 52,000lb tractive effort from their 215lb boilers and 22in cylinders. Even more American in appearance were the twelve 4-8-4s of Class 520 turned out from the road's Islington shops in 1943-47; styled after the Pennsylvania's duplex-drive T1s, the 520s would have looked equally at home in Harrisburg or Fort Wayne. South Australia's 3ft 6in gauge lines also boasted some impressive steam power, including Australian-designed Garratts and ten 4-8-2 + 2-8-4s delivered by Société Franco-Belge in 1953.

A year earlier Victoria, too, was taking delivery of a major new steam design—the 70 big Class R express-passenger Hudsons built by North British; production of Victorian Railways' Class J 2-8-0s continued until 1954. Superpower in no small measure was provided by New South Wales Government Railways' AD.60 class Garratts, also of 1952 vintage, that were the southern hemisphere's most powerful standard-gauge steam locomotives. Sampling footplate travel on these immense 4-8-4 + 4-8-4s, as I did on 6006 heading a 1500-ton coal train from Glenlee Colliery to the Sydney Harbour coal docks at Rozelle, recalled the days of Norfolk & Western Y6s and Chesapeake & Ohio H8s hauling Appalachian coal down to Virginia's Hampton Roads.

1200 miles across the Tasman Sea, New Zealand steam power was of more modest dimensions. Beyer-Garratts there proved unsuccessful and were converted to Pacifics; most advanced steam locomotives were the K and Ka class 4-8-4s and their postwar Ja 4-8-2 counterparts that remained in service until the early 1970s.

New Zealand's last steam-powered main-line express, the 'South Island Limited' hammers upgrade out of Christchurch on the first leg of its 388-mile journey to Invercargill. Motive power on this crisp autumn morning in 1967 is Ja class 4-8-2 No. 1253.

Experience with Beyer-Garratts in Australia was never as satisfactory as on the narrow-gauge railways of Africa, and the decision of NSWGR engineers to buy sixty 4-8-4 + 4-8-4s from Beyer Peacock as late as 1952 was widely criticised at the time. In the event, though only 42 complete engines and eight assemblies were imported, they quickly won a high reputation, and were among the final steam locomotives to meet the cutting torch.

The big stoker-fired Garratts, weighing 260 tons, had a tractive effort of 63,000lb—greater than that of any standard-gauge steam engine in the southern hemisphere. By the late 1960's, as NSW freight services were increasingly turned over to diesel and electric traction, most of the Garratts were concentrated at Broadmeadow depot, Newcastle; an exception was 6006—here photographed at Campbelltown on an autumn afternoon in 1967—and two sister engines, retained at Enfield to handle the heavy Glenlee-Rozelle coal trains.

Two eras of Victorian Railways' steam power rest side-by-side at Newport shops in May 1967. 635 is a D3 class mixed-traffic 4-6-0 of 1929, double-stacked 220 a unique three-cylinder 4-8-4 built at Newport in 1941. Tractive force of 55,000lb was unjustified in VR operation, and 220 remained the only representative of her type.

The late 1960's saw steam operation drawing to a close in New South Wales: that remaining was kept in impeccable condition, as evidenced by Class C38 Pacific 3828 at Enfield, Sydney, in the autumn of 1967. Designed by NSWGR Chief Mechanical Engineer H. Young, five streamlined C38s entered service in 1945; 25 more emerged from Cardiff and Eveleigh shops between then and 1948.

Zenith of steam locomotive design in New Zealand was the Ja class 4-8-2. Hillside shops, ▷ Dunedin, turned out 35 of the type between 1946 and 1956, all for use in the South Island; 16 oil-fired variants for the North Island were supplied by North British in 1952. Coal-burner 1253 is being readied for service at Christchurch in April 1967.

Among the last steam locomotives to be built by Baldwin, the 20 Mikados of New South Wales Railways' Class D59 were shipped from Philadelphia in 1952. Originally oil-fired, several were later converted to burn coal. Most lasted until the late 1960's; 5910 was photographed on a northbound freight near Campbelltown during her last week of service.

Two C38 Pacifics on the ready track at Enfield depot, Sydney. On this autumn morning in 1967, 3828 has brought in the 'Southern Highlands Express'; 3808 is booked for a freight to Moss Vale.

Victorian Railways' broad-gauge R.723 represents the only Australian class of express-passenger 4-6-4. The stoker-fired Hudson came from North British in 1952.

NSWGR 3675, below, outlasted many of the Pacifics that followed. She is one of 75 C36-class 4-6-0s built in 1925-28 by Clyde Engineering and the road's Eveleigh shops.

Though few of the locomotives illustrated in this book saw service into the 1970's, surprisingly many can be found in museums throughout the world. Among them, and a fitting finale to the story of steam superpower, is one of the unique Lima-built 2-6-6-6 simple articulateds designed in 1941 for the Chesapeake & Ohio. 45 were built that year, a further 15 in 1949; they could handle 12,000-ton trains at 45 mile/h and achieve power outputs of more than 8000 ihp.

Numbered 1600 to 1659, the H8s spent their brief lives heading vast coal trains through the Alleghenies. Despite the unlimited supply of cheap coal, diesel power began to replace steam in the early 1950s, and soon the last of the H8s, in some cases after a working life of only five years, were withdrawn for scrapping. Today, 1601 rests in the Henry Ford Museum at Greenfield Village, Michigan.